P9-BZY-300

HOW CAN I EXPERIMENT WITH ... ?

A WHEEL

David and Patricia Armentrout

Rourke
Publishing LLC
Vero Beach, Florida 32964

www.rourkepublishing.com

PHOTO CREDITS: ©Armentrout pgs 13, 17, 23; ©James P. Rowan pgs 4, 7; ©David French Photography pgs 15, 19, 20, 25, 27, 29; ©Image 100 Ltd. Cover, pg 11; ©PhotoDisc pg 9.

Cover: *Some say the wheel is humankind's greatest invention.*

Editor: Frank Sloan

Cover design: Nicola Stratford

Series Consulting Editor: Henry Rasof, a former editor with Franklin Watts, has edited many science books for children and young adults.

Library of Congress Cataloging-in-Publication Data

Armentrout, David, 1962-
  How can I experiment with simple machines? A wheel / David and
Patricia Armentrout.
      p. cm.
Summary: Defines wheels, explains their functions, and suggests simple
experiments to demonstrate how they work.
Includes bibliographical references and index.
  ISBN 1-58952-338-5
  1. Wheels—Juvenile literature. [1. Wheels—Experiments. 2.
Experiments.] I. Title: Wheel. II. Armentrout, Patricia, 1960- III.
Title.
  TJ181.5 .A758 2002
  621.8—dc21

                                                    2002007950

Printed in the USA

W/W

Table of Contents

Wheel (WEEL) — a round disk or object that turns on an axle; a simple machine that makes work easier

A ferris wheel is a giant wheel and axle powered by a motor.

5

Simple Machines

For thousands of years people lived without modern machines. There were no refrigerators to keep food fresh. No one had cars to travel in. And there were no telephones or radios for communication. However, people did use machines. They used simple machines.

The wheel, the pulley, the wedge, the lever, the inclined plane, and the screw are simple machines. They are the basis of all other machines.

Water wheels were once used to provide power for mills.

Wheel and Axle

Some say the wheel is humankind's greatest invention. The wheel gives us a **mechanical advantage**. This means the wheel helps us do more work with less effort.

An **axle** is a shaft in the center of the wheel. The wheel turns with, or around, the axle. Without the wheel and axle, we would not have cars, bikes, or skateboards. Wheels are so common that modern life would be impossible without them.

Cars, bikes, and many other machines would not be possible without the wheel and axle.

Friction

Do you have any idea why wheels were invented in the first place? It all has to do with **friction**. Friction is a force that happens when two objects are rubbed together. Friction can slow movement.

Think about friction. What happens when you scuff your feet on the ground as you walk? You go slower, right? The friction between your shoes and the ground slows your movement.

Friction helps win a game of tug-of-war.

Experiment with Friction

You will need:

- friend
- gentle-sloped street away from traffic
- pair of roller skates

Go to the top of the slope with your friend. Have your friend stand facing downhill. Put on your skates. Stand facing downhill next to your friend. What happens?

Did you have trouble staying at the top? Did the wheels on your skates make it easier for you to move? How about your friend? Did your friend move? Of course not—your friend had friction. You had wheels. The wheels reduced the friction and helped you move downhill.

It is hard to keep from moving when there are wheels under your feet.

Experiment with Friction and Bearings

Some machines have a lot of moving parts. Small balls made of metal or other materials, called **bearings**, are placed between moving parts to reduce friction. Bearings are in the wheels of skateboards and roller skates. See how bearings reduce friction in wheels.

You will need:

- marbles
- paint can
- heavy book

Space some of the marbles evenly around the lip of the paint can. Imagine this is a wheel with bearings. Now, place the book on top of the bearings. Push the edge of the book. Did the bearings help the book move freely?

Ball bearings reduce friction between the moving parts of a machine.

15

Wheel Size

What do roller skate wheels, bicycle wheels, and tractor wheels have in common? If you said they are all round you are right. All wheels are round, but they are not all the same size. Machines come in all sizes, so wheels have to, also.

What would happen if you put roller skate wheels on a car? To cover the same distance, small wheels have to turn more times than larger wheels have to. Large wheels have a greater mechanical advantage—they can cover a greater distance with less effort.

Wheels are made to fit different-sized machines.

Experiment with Wheel Size

You will need:

- masking tape
- toy car with small wheels
- toy car with large wheels
- poster board
- pencil

Use the masking tape to mark a line on the bottom of the front wheels of each car. Place the poster board on the floor. Set the cars, with the front wheels at one end of the board, facing the opposite end of the board. Make sure the wheels are turned so that the tape touches the board.

Mark the wheels with tape to make it easy to count the number of turns the wheels make.

Small wheels have to turn more times to cover the same distance as larger wheels.

Slowly roll one car forward until the tape makes one complete turn and touches the board again. Use the pencil to mark that spot on the poster board. Continue the process until your car reaches the end of the board.

Do the same thing with the second car. Count the number of marks for each car. Which car made the most turns, the small-wheeled car or the large-wheeled car?

Gears

A gear is made up of at least two wheels with teeth. The teeth on one wheel fit between the teeth of another, linking them together. Because the teeth are linked, turning one wheel causes the other wheel to turn.

Gears give us a mechanical advantage, too. Gears transfer movement from one part of a machine to another. Gears can also change the speed and direction of movement.

Mechanical clocks and watches have gears. Egg beaters, bikes, and cars have gears. Can you think of any machines with gears?

This bike has a special system that moves the chain from one gear to another.

Make Your Own Gears

You will need:

- small plate
- drinking glass
- pencil
- paper
- scissors
- 28 craft sticks
- glue
- paper fasteners
- poster board

With the plate and drinking glass as guides, use the pencil to trace two large and one small circle on the paper. Cut out the circles. Place 12 of the craft sticks on each large circle. Space them evenly, forming a wheel with spokes. Leave a space in the center and about 2 inches (5 centimeters) of the sticks hanging off the circle's edge. Glue the sticks in place.

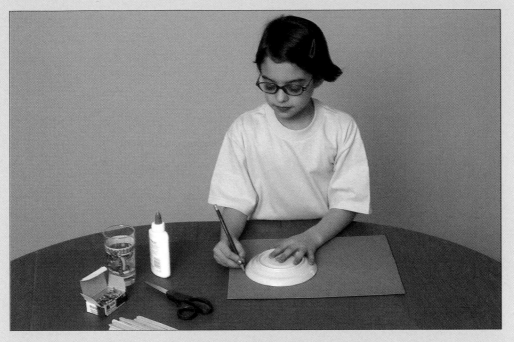

Trace around the plate and glass to make your circles.

Glue craft sticks to the circles to make gear teeth.

25

Gently break the remaining four craft sticks in half. Place the eight pieces on the small circle in the same way you did for the large gears. Glue the sticks in place. Set the small gear aside to use later.

Using paper fasteners for axles, attach the two large wheels to the poster board. Make sure the teeth are linked and the gears move freely on their axles.

Gently turn one gear clockwise. What happens to the other gear? When you turn one gear clockwise the second moves counterclockwise. This type of gear transfers movement from one direction to another.

Use paper fasteners to attach your gears to the poster board.

Turning one gear clockwise will cause the other gear to move counterclockwise.

27

Gears and Speed

Gears can change the direction of movement, but can gears control the speed of the movement?

Remove one large gear from the poster board and replace it with the small gear. Make sure the teeth are close enough to be linked, and the gears move freely on their axles. You now have gears of different sizes.

Gently turn the large gear one complete turn. What happens to the small gear? Does it turn more than once? When two wheels of different sizes are linked, the larger wheel will turn more slowly than the smaller wheel. This type of gear changes the speed of movement.

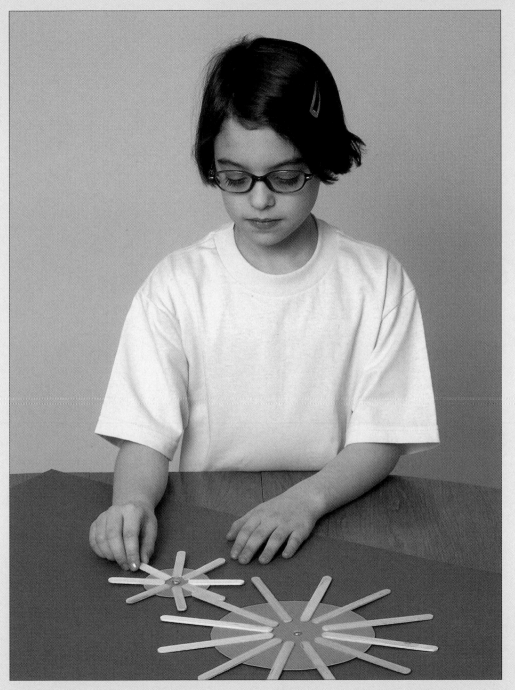

When two gears of different sizes are linked, the smaller gear will turn faster than the larger gear.

Glossary

axle (AK sul) — a shaft on which a wheel turns

bearings (BAIR ingz) — balls placed between moving parts of machines to reduce friction

friction (FRIK shun) — a force that slows two objects when they are rubbed together

gears (GEERZ) — wheels with teeth that are connected together

mechanical advantage (mi KAN eh kul ad VAN tij) — what you gain when a simple machine allows you to use less effort

Further Reading

Macaulay, David. *The New Way Things Work.* Houghton Mifflin Company, 1998

Seller, Mick. *Wheels, Pulleys & Levers.* Gloucester Press, 1993

VanCleave, Janice. *Machines.* John Wiley & Sons, Inc., 1993

Websites to Visit

http://www.kidskonnect.com/SimpleMachines/ SimpleMachinesHome.html

http://www.mos.org/sin/Leonardo/ InventorsToolbox.html

http://www.brainpop.com/tech/simplemachines/

Index

About the Authors

David and Patricia Armentrout have written many nonfiction books for young readers. They specialize in science and social studies topics. They have had several books published for primary school reading. The Armentrouts live in Cincinnati, Ohio, with their two children.